O9-BTO-391

PRAYERS
AND OTHER RESOURCES
FOR PUBLIC WORSHIP

PRAYERS
AND OTHER RESOURCES
FOR PUBLIC WORSHIP

Horton Davies ● **Morris Slifer**

ABINGDON

NASHVILLE

Prayers and Other Resources for Public Worship

Copyright © 1976 by Abingdon
Second Printing 1978 ·

Library of Congress Cataloging in Publication Data

1. Prayers. I. Davies, Horton. II. Slifer, Morris D., 1904-
BV245.P82   264' .1   76-23251

ISBN 0-687-33495-0

MANUFACTURED BY THE PARTHENON PRESS AT
NASHVILLE, TENNESSEE, UNITED STATES OF AMERICA

CONTENTS

INTRODUCTION

The separation of church(es) and state in the United States of America has had the effect of letting each religious community worship in its own way, resulting in great variety and sincerity in worship. It has also occasionally led to much disorderliness and irreverence in divine devotions.

It is our hope that this anthology of public prayers and other resources will be used both by congregations usually using a liturgy and by those who rely for freshness on their ministers' conceiving their own prayers. These resources should supplement the uniformity, universality, dignity, and fidelity to tradition which characterize a liturgy, with the contemporaneity, relevance, novelty, and intimacy which characterize prayers composed by pastors who know their people well. They may also, we trust, assist ministers to vary their pastoral prayers by the use of new resources.

The two editors are ministers of the United Church of Christ who have served for many years on its Commission on Worship, and many of the prayers are the original compositions of the clergy of that Church, while some of the invitatory sentences from Scripture have been selected by them. But the acknowledgments at the end of the book will prove that we have ranged widely throughout the English-speaking world to find additional resources for worship.

The table of contents will show the variety of worship

materials we have assembled. The unusualness of our book consists in this: here alone, so far as we know, there are collated all the materials used in public worship and supplied within the covers of one book. The book includes a great variety of prayers, such as prayers of invocation, prayers for illumination (to be used prior to lections and sermons), prayers for the church year, bidding prayers, offertory prayers, prayers of confession, general prayers, and prayers for special occasions and special graces. It also includes sentences of Scripture for use at the opening of the service and at the offertory, confessions of sin and declarations of pardon, blessings, benedictions and dismissals—in short, all the elements contained in an order of worship.

In our selection of resources we have tried to keep in mind the following criteria. We wanted these resources to be thoroughly biblical, reverent in spirit and expression (avoiding all meretricious slickness and superficiality), simple, honest, and contemporary. Our resources are themselves a fruit of the liturgical movement, which has made giant steps of progress in our times, and we should like to draw particular attention to the admirable eucharistic prayer of consecration, selected from a British Baptist source. Of churches, as well as of individual church members, we can say, "We are members of one another."

As we send out this volume of prayers and other resources for worship, we pray that they may be used for the greater glory of God, for the greater expression of the unity of Christ's church, and for the criticism and comfort of God's people.

HORTON DAVIES
MORRIS SLIFER

OPENING SENTENCES

ADVENT

Blessed be the Lord God of Israel,
for he has visited and redeemed his people,
and has raised up a horn of salvation for us
in the house of his servant David,
through the tender mercy of our God,
when the day shall dawn upon us from on high
to give light to those who sit in darkness and in the
  shadow of death,
to guide our feet into the way of peace.

(Luke 1:68, 69, 78, 79)

CHRISTMAS

Behold, the dwelling of God is with men.
He will dwell with them, and they shall be his people,
and God himself will be with them.

(Revelation 21:3)

LAST SUNDAY OF THE YEAR

I am sure that neither death, nor life, nor angels,
nor principalities, nor things present, nor things to
  come,
nor powers, nor height, nor depth, nor anything else in
  all creation,
will be able to separate us from the love of God in Christ
  Jesus our Lord.   *(Romans 8:38, 39)*

NEW YEAR

And he who sat upon the throne said, "Behold, I make
all things new." Also he said, "Write this, for these

9

words are trustworthy and true." And he said to me, "It is done! I am the Alpha and the Omega, the beginning and the end. To the thirsty I will give from the fountain of the water of life without payment.

(Revelation 21:5, 6)

EPIPHANY AND AFTER

In many and various ways God spoke of old to our
    fathers by the prophets;
but in these last days he has spoken to us by a Son . . .
He reflects the glory of God and bears the very stamp of
    his nature.   *(Hebrews 1:1, 2, 3)*

LENT

Therefore, since we are surrounded by so great a cloud of witnesses, let us also lay aside every weight, and sin which clings so closely, and let us run with perseverance the race that is set before us, looking to Jesus the pioneer and perfecter of our faith, who for the joy that was set before him endured the cross, despising the shame, and is seated at the right hand of the throne of God.   *(Hebrews 12:1, 2)*

MAUNDY THURSDAY

Christ, our paschal lamb, has been sacrificed. Let us, therefore, celebrate the festival, not with the old leaven, the leaven of malice and evil, but with the unleavened bread of sincerity and truth.   *(I Corinthians 5:7, 8)*

EASTER

The gospel of God which he promised beforehand through his prophets in the holy scriptures, the gospel concerning his Son, who was descended from David according to the flesh and designated Son of God in power according to the Spirit of holiness by his resurrection from the dead, Jesus Christ our Lord.

(Romans 1:2-4)

SUNDAY AFTER EASTER

As Christ was raised from the dead by the glory of the Father, we too might walk in newness of life.

(Romans 6:4)

You have been born anew, not of perishable seed but of imperishable, through the living and abiding word of God.
That word is the good news which was preached to you.

(I Peter 1:23, 25)

PENTECOST

God's love has been poured into our hearts through the Holy Spirit which has been given to us. For all who are led by the Spirit of God are sons of God. It is the Spirit himself bearing witness with our spirit that we are children of God.   *(Romans 5:5; 8:14, 16)*

LOYALTY SUNDAY

I appeal to you therefore, brethren, by the mercies of God, to present your bodies as a living sacrifice, holy and acceptable to God, which is your spiritual worship.

(Romans 12:1)

THANKSGIVING

Let the peoples praise thee, O God;
    let all the peoples praise thee!

11

The earth has yielded its increase;
   God, our God, has blessed us.
God has blessed us;
   let all the ends of the earth fear him!

(Psalm 67:5-7)

COMMUNION

Behold, I stand at the door and knock; if any one hears
my voice and opens the door, I will come in to him and
eat with him, and he with me.   *(Revelation 3:20)*

GENERAL

Blessed be the name of God for ever and ever,
   to whom belong wisdom and might.
He changes times and seasons;
   he removes kings and sets up kings;
he gives wisdom to the wise
   and knowledge to those who have understanding;
he reveals deep and mysterious things;
   he knows what is in the darkness,
   and the light dwells with him.   *(Daniel 2:20-22)*

Make a joyful noise to God, all the earth;
   sing the glory of his name;
   give to him glorious praise!
Bless our God, O peoples,
   let the sound of his praise be heard,
who has kept us among the living,
   and has not let our feet slip.   *(Psalm 66:1, 2, 8, 9)*

Blessed be the Lord,
   who daily bears us up;
   God is our salvation.

Ascribe power to God,
 whose majesty is over Israel,
 and his power is in the skies.
Terrible is God in his sanctuary,
 the God of Israel,
 he gives power and strength to his people.
Blessed be God!   *(Psalm 68:19, 34, 35)*

Great and wonderful are thy deeds,
O Lord God the Almighty!
Just and true are thy ways,
O King of the ages!
Who shall not fear and glorify thy name, O Lord?
For thou alone art holy.
All nations shall come and worship thee,
for thy judgments have been revealed.
       (Revelation 15:3-4)

PRAYERS OF INVOCATION

1. To whom may we turn for life, but to you, O God, for you are the God of the living; and to whom may we go for guidance, but to your Son, for he has the words of Eternal Life.

Once again, in this act of worship, you have provided us with the opportunity of experiencing our kinship with you, and with all who worship you in heaven and on earth.

In your presence we rejoice, for by it our lives are given significance, and through it the passing moments are enriched. Lead us in your way, O Father, through Jesus Christ our Lord. *Amen.*

2. We pause, O Lord, in the midst of our frantic business and our prideful activities, to approach you. Help us to be sincere in our approach, that we may come before you in reverence and awe; and worship you in spirit and in truth.

Startle us into life that we may be ready to receive new flashes of understanding, and have our eyes opened to behold your wonder and your glory. Turn us to yourself that we may turn from death to the joy of life, through Jesus Christ our Lord. *Amen.*

3. We come to you, O Father Eternal, recognizing that you have created us to seek you, to love you, and to find our identity within the fellowship of your faithful

people. Help us so to participate in this service of praise and thanksgiving, offered to you as our reasonable service, that we may be opened to receive from you new gifts of grace, new glimpses of truth, and a deeper experience of the life you have given us, through Jesus Christ our Lord. *Amen.*

4. Open the eyes of our faith, O God, for we have failed to see the evidences of your handiwork, and we have missed your glory. Help us to see the light in our darkness, the beauty which transcends ugliness, the flower on the garbage heap, the brother within each neighbor, the Eternal entering time, and your kingdom close at hand. Help us to look honestly at ourselves and at the idols we worship, that we may see ourselves and our chosen values for what they are. Bless this time of quiet, reflection, prayer, and praise, that it may be a time of commitment to you through Jesus Christ our Lord. *Amen.*

5. We come before you, O God, our Father, acknowledging in honesty that so often we look upon you as an old-fashioned and out-of-date deity. We do not think that you are quite up to our standards, or that we need to depend upon you for anything. Bless us with your presence, and encourage us with your compassion to look at ourselves anew and to see ourselves as we truly are, stripped of our pride, our pretensions, and our follies. Help us to look away from ourselves; free us from our spiritual blindness; that we may see you in the holiness of your love, and in the truth made known to us by the Holy Spirit who unites us with you and one another, through Jesus Christ our Lord. *Amen.*

15

6. Eternal Father, we need to come away from the pressures and the anxieties of everyday existence, to be with you, to be with your people, and to be honest with ourselves. We thank you that you speak not only in the tumultuous noise and anger of our times, but also in the silences—silences we hear so seldom because we are too involved in the noises.

Grant us a moment of freedom, a moment of insight, a moment of grace, a moment of wisdom that we may return to the arena of daily existence strengthened in spirit, renewed in compassion, and ready to do your will, through Jesus Christ our Lord. *Amen.*

7. We remember, O Lord, how your Son set his face resolutely in the direction of Jerusalem to complete the work you had given him to do. Strengthen us, therefore, by your love, that we may finish our tasks faithfully and joyfully, whatever they may be. Help us to remember that we are human beings, and that you are always calling us to be more human. May we see the difference between what is admired by you and by public opinion, and rejoice in that difference, through Jesus Christ our Lord. *Amen.*

8. We rejoice, O Father, with great joy, for you have brought us into fellowship with yourself in the life eternal. By giving us your life you have given glory to our daily existence. Wherever we are, we are never absent, nor far away, from you. Life in your presence is good, and the comradeship of your people is thrilling. By our worship in the fellowship of love may we enter into the fullness of life, and may our hearts glow warmly from the joy of being with you, through Jesus Christ our Lord. *Amen.*

9. Father, we realize that we need to be forgiven, not because you condemn us, but because we condemn ourselves, love our guilt, and miss your glory. Help us to be happy in the freedom that is ours; freedom from past guilt, and from old well-worn convenient sins. Help us to infect others with the contagion of our own joy, and not to be upset when it is rejected or missed or used in evidence against us. Glory be to you, through Jesus Christ our Lord. *Amen.*

10. We thank you, O Father, for preparing a road through our wilderness, for revealing that way to us through your Son and for supplying all our needs, but above all, the needs of our souls; for initiating a discussion with us; and for challenging us to seek ever-expanding frontiers. So often we experience dryness of spirit, joylessness of heart, and weakness of will. We come to you now, because you have come to us with the gift of life. We rejoice in your goodness, and praise you for the hope given to us through the Resurrection, and through your Son, our Brother, even Jesus Christ our Lord. *Amen.*

11. We have come here, O God, our Father, to learn a little more of the mystery which your Son made known to us. We rejoice that he is the Teacher you sent to instruct us in the deep things of the spirit. By his experience as a man, by his compassionate suffering, by his triumphant living and dying, he opened a way for every man, a way which leads to your heart of love. In this service help us to remember that we are following your ascending Son who is constantly leading us on toward greater experiences in truth, and greater

adventures in love. Teach us, O Father, for we have so much to learn, through Jesus Christ our Lord. *Amen.*

12. O Lord, our God, like Martha we are anxious about many things; we are so cluttered up with the burdens of this world that we are hardly even able to recognize you as the living God of Abraham, Isaac, Jacob, and of our fathers who have loved and served you in their generations. Yet in this time of worship we dare to turn away from ourselves and our exaggerated problems, to be still in your presence, and by the spirit of adoption to call you, not Lord, but Father. Open the eyes of our faith that we may see you, our ears that we may hear you, and our hearts that we may love you. *Amen.*

13. We come to you, O Father, not because we must, but because we may. We come in freedom to praise you, and to find our place in life as human beings, created from dust, yet called to be men and women of spirit. Our lives have, as their context, the turmoil of violence, the frustration of uncertainty, and the anguish of the suffering of the innocent. Touch us by your Spirit that we may be keenly sensitive to the needs of our times, and brave enough to respond to them according to our talents and ability; through Jesus Christ our Lord. *Amen.*

14. We come before you, Lord,
bringing our intentions and our hopes;
bringing too our doubts and fears;
bringing as our overriding prayers
the wants and the desires

that we can never put aside for long.
Take us as we are, Lord,
and help us in the act of worship
to be honest with ourselves;
to put aside our virtuous pretensions
and to know for certain
that your love for us expressed through
   Jesus Christ
will more than make up for our faults
if only we will stop pretending
and let you use us as you will
and not as we decide may be convenient. *Amen*.

15. Pull us together, Lord.
Pull each of us together
from the scattered pieces
that our distracted way of life
has flung about the landscape of our minds
until our vision blurs
and our attention span is cut to zero.
Pull us together, Lord.
Pull all of us together
from the conflicts and the fears
that cause us to suspect each other's motives
and to withhold our trust.
Pull us together, each and all,
by your example and your Word
and by your Spirit
which you have put among us
for all time
in the person and the presence
of Jesus Christ our Lord. *Amen*.

16. We stand in poverty before your riches, Lord.
We are in ignorance before your total wisdom.
Our moments tick away too fast
for us to contemplate eternity.
We are afraid to think too much about you,
Especially are we afraid to think
of what your justice might require.
Come to us, Lord.
Come not only from the direction
in which we look for you.
But come upon us from our blind side,
And surprise us with your joy. *Amen.*

CONFESSIONS OF SIN

17. Our God, whose Son is the light of the world,
   in his penetrating light we acknowledge our
      darkness;
   in his constant grace our careless love;
   in his generous giving our sordid grasping;
   in his equal justice our dire prejudice;
   in his fortitude our fearful failure;
   in his inclusive love our deep divisions;
   in his pure sacrifice our soiling sins.
But in his cross is our forgiveness,
and in his resurrection our enduring hope.
The pardon and the promise now we claim,
in penitence and faith, through Jesus Christ our Lord.
Amen.

18. We claim thee, God, and claim thy promises.
So now, we bow in sad awareness of
Our sins: our hate, our prejudice, our greed,
Our laziness and sloth; our coward's way
When truth or justice, mercy and a sharing
Love are called for day by day. Forgive,
We pray. Thou Lord of Lords and King of Kings,
Thou Babe in time and Prince of Peace eternal:
Thou'rt God come down to save us! We are here
to claim in boldness all that saving grace,
And wait with hearts low-bowed before thy face. *Amen.*

19. Almighty and most merciful God, our heavenly
Father, we humble ourselves before you, under a deep

sense of our unworthiness and guilt. We have griev-
ously sinned against you, in thought, in word, and in
deed. We have come short of your glory, we have
broken your commandments, and have turned aside
from the way of life. Yet now, most merciful Father,
hear us when we call upon you with penitent hearts,
and for the sake of your Son, Jesus Christ, have mercy
upon us. Pardon our sins; take away our guilt; and
grant us your peace. Purify us, by the inspiration of
your Holy Spirit, from all inward uncleanness, and
make us able and willing to serve you in newness of life,
to the glory of your holy Name, through Jesus Christ
our Lord. *Amen.*

Used by permission of Eden Publishing House.

20. Forgive us, Judge of all the earth,
for we content ourselves with words
And do not make them good with deeds.
We call Christ Lord but serve him not.
We call him Light but live in shadows.
We say he is The Way but do not follow.
Have mercy on us, God
Forgive us who confess our faults,
Restoring those who turn again,
According to the promises
your Son, our Lord, declared. *Amen.*

21. O God of truth and fact,
forgive us for the myths we generate:
about our heritage, to falsify the past;
about ourselves, to hide our present faults;
about those strange to us, to justify our lack of charity.
Give us courage to seek and to face all truth;

give us humility to see with less distortion;
and give us grace to act upon the truth your Spirit
  leads us to perceive. *Amen.*

22. O God, forgive us for the way we sanctify
    advantages, and
elevate our private good to heaven.
We make our way of life the test of all societies and
  scorn all other styles.
We seek your blessing and avoid your judgment,
  and make you in the image of our wish.
For our presumptions, Lord, have mercy on us all.
Amen.

23. Forgive us, Lord, the mockery we make of grace
    and truth,
  goodwill and peace in Jesus' advent time.
We confess the vulgar festival: the scheming gifts,
  the bounded love, the sentimental song,
  the lavish ostentation
while inns are full and stables are ignored.
The homeless wander in the night, and innocents
  are slain by our neglect.
Forgive us, Lord. *Amen.*

24. As we mark the season of remembrance of the
life and passion of our Lord, we pray you, Father,
forgive us our offenses, and cleanse us from our sins of
doing wrong and failing to do good. Heal us, but with
the painful understanding of how our own hands nail
the Son of God to the cross again, exposing him to
public shame. Show us the hurt by which our hands
have crucified your Son, and through that hurting heal
us. *Amen.*

23

25. O God whose apostle taught that we must die to sin before we can be raised to live a new life, if we have come before you here with garments changed but with our hearts the same, and with the power of sin still in command, we ask that you will teach us the lesson of the cross, that we may truly come alive in the power of the resurrection. *Amen.*

26. New life stirs and springs up all around us, Lord; while we are earthbound still,
disabled, dull, held down by doubts, kept back by fears,
ashamed of what we fail to do, appalled at what we've done.
Forgive us, Lord.
Renew us in the resurrection light
as once it shone for Peter, John, and Mary Magdalene.
Transform our weakness by your strength that we may be
alive to Christ and to the lives of those you've given us to serve. *Amen.*

27. Our Father, whose Son prayed that all his disciples might be one; we acknowledge our part in the guilt of schism—in helping to split and splinter the one church into a multitude of denominations and sects; we confess that we pray to Christ from competitive altars and preach his Word from rival pulpits; we admit that the beating of the denominational drum drowns out the symphony of praise; unite us, O God, by the power of your Holy Spirit, who is the very bond of charity. *Amen.*

28. God of all nations and people; we confess before you our racial arrogance and prejudice, that foments

riots and lynchings, insults and injuries; we confess that our love of our neighbor is often less than skin deep, and that our false pride endangers the safety and unity of the human race; enable us with the compassionate eyes of Christ to be wholly color-blind and to recognize in all men and women your image and the dignity of those for whom Christ died; through the same Jesus Christ, our Lord. *Amen.*

29. O God, whose beloved Son was placed in a borrowed grave; we confess that our affluent society has left us rich in possessions, penny-pinching in generosity, and bankrupt in social justice; bring us by our Savior's warnings to repentance, and by the example of his simplicity of life enable us to seek the Kingdom without caste, whose ruler is Christ our Lord. *Amen.*

30. Almighty God, our Father, we are surrounded by human need on every hand. Sometimes we shelter ourselves from those who are in need, pretending they do not exist. Sometimes we harden our hearts, because we cannot bear to see others suffer. Forgive us this insensitivity. Fill our hearts with the compassion of Christ, that we may be agents in your hands to heal the hurts of the world; through Jesus Christ our Lord. *Amen.*

31. O God, you have sent your son Jesus to us, so that we may know the truth that sets us free. In him we know the way, the truth and the life. We confess before you that we have not always followed that way, lived in his truth, or accepted the life he offers to us. Having

eyes, we preferred not to see; having ears, we pretended
not to hear. Forgive us, O God, for our self-deception.
Open us to the indwelling of your Spirit, that your truth
may take possession of us; through Christ our Lord.
Amen.

32. Have mercy upon us, O God,
according to your loving-kindness.
According to your abundant mercy
blot out our transgressions.
Wash us thoroughly from our iniquity,
And cleanse us from our sin.
Create in us a clean heart, O God,
and renew in us a right spirit.
Cast us not away from your presence,
and take not your holy Spirit from us.
Restore to us the joy of your salvation,
and uphold us with a willing spirit.

33. Most holy and merciful Father,
we confess to you and to one another,
and to the whole communion of saints in heaven and
earth.
that we have sinned against you
by what we have done,
and by what we have left undone.
We have not loved you with our whole heart and mind
and strength,
We have not loved our neighbors as ourselves,
We have not had in us the mind of Christ,
We have grieved your Holy Spirit.
You alone know how often we have sinned and grieved
you,

by wasting your gifts,
by wandering from your ways,
by forgetting your love.
Forgive us, we pray you, most merciful Father,
and free us from our sin,
Renew in us again the grace and strength of your Holy
Spirit,
for the sake of Jesus Christ, your Son our
Savior *Amen.*

34. Almighty and gracious God, Creator and Judge of
all men,
Father of our Lord Jesus Christ:
We acknowledge and confess our many sins
which we have committed by thought, word, and deed,
against you and our neighbors.
Have mercy on us for the sake of your Son our Savior.
Forgive us all our sins and offenses,
and strengthen us by your Holy Spirit:
That we may hereafter love and serve you in newness of
life,
to the honor and glory of your Name;
through Jesus Christ our Lord. *Amen.*

35. O God of purity and compassion, dispel the
coldness and callousness of our hearts, that like the
penitent prodigal we may come to ourselves, and like
remorseful Peter we may mourn our denials and find
ourselves reconciled in Jesus Christ our Lord. *Amen.*

36. Most Holy God, before whose presence the guilty
flee as clouds before the sun, in the light of your love we
confess the darkness of our desires and the deviousness

of our deeds; we are without excuse or reason, and we plead only our need of your forgiveness promised in Jesus Christ our Lord. *Amen.*

37. Lord God, whose will is to establish one universal kingdom and family for all mankind, forgive us for the feuds that ruin friendships, for the pride that differentiates between rich and poor, between black and white, between denomination and sect, differences which we accentuate instead of overcoming; and give us the power of reconciliation in Christ, your Son and friend of all forever. *Amen.*

38. O God, you know our desperate need for your gift of understanding and forgiveness in order to live in harmony with our neighbors. You know how repeatedly and how hopelessly we forget your love for us, and turn back continually to ourselves as though your love were not to be trusted. We confess that we have nourished grievances and irritations which we ought to forgive; we have sinfully thought our differences too great for reconciliation; and our community is wounded by our selfishness, prejudice and pride. . . . Since you are love, and the source of all love, give us strength to leave the easy path of self-satisfaction; grant us the courage to forgive as we hope to be forgiven; and in your mercy heal our divisions and make us whole, together, in the love which we have from you; through Jesus Christ our Lord. *Amen.*

39. Forgive us, Lord, for our participation in those built-in systems, wrongs from which we cannot separate ourselves because they are based on privilege,

because our nation is powerful, because our wealth is relatively great; because our heritage is favored, because the prejudice of others, if not indeed our own, restricts our neighborhoods; because we are protected by forces we do not control. Help us to reach out further in reconciliation. And let us not assume that our virtues are not burdensome to others, we pray in Jesus' name. *Amen.*

40. O God, forgive our pretense of self-sufficiency, our claim to be in control of our destinies, and our pride in thinking that we live decent and honorable lives. Help us to face and overcome our ignorance of the human need that our relative wealth and influence could help to meet, our evasion of responsibility for wrong because we know that righting it would change our way of life, and most of all our indifference to the suffering of others. We pray in Jesus' name. *Amen.*

41. O God, we do not really want to look honestly at our lives, to admit our weaknesses and to confess our sins. Life is so complicated, Lord; we are confused. We do not know how to choose when all the alternatives are both good and evil. Forgive us the evil we do while trying to do good. We are so selfish, God. We do not want to bear others' burdens as well as our own. Forgive us our attempts to escape the responsibility of belonging to one another in your whole human family. Hear our prayer, O God of mercy. *Amen.*

42. O Lord most holy and righteous,
We acknowledge before you that we do not fear you as
    we should,

And that we do not love you above all else.

We do not delight in prayer and we run away from your Word.

We do not love our neighbors;

And we are too much interested in ourselves;

We are vain, irritable, and full of pride.

We are lacking in private conscience and public concern;

We take advantage of others and their work.

Our hearts are divided, paralyzed by doubts and guilty desires.

We bring our shabby selves before you, God;

Forgive us, cleanse us, and clothe us with newness of life;

Through Jesus Christ our Lord. *Amen.*

43. God of mercy and of healing, help us to confess our sin against you and against our neighbors. We choose the easy wrong rather than the hard right; we prefer to walk in darkness rather than light; we would rather enjoy our sins than bare them before you. Search us, O God, and know us. Create in us clean hearts; for between our sins and their rewards we would set the sacrifice of Christ our Lord. *Amen.*

44. O Lord our God, pardon and forgive all the sins we have committed knowingly or through ignorance, whether by word or deed: absolve us, we pray you, for you are good and gracious; and make us fit to be members of your body and temples of your Holy Spirit, through Jesus Christ our Lord. *Amen.*

45. O Lord our God, you are our Father, and we are your children: We confess that we are wicked and

disobedient, always seeking our own way. In our family life we have neglected you; in our working life we have forgotten you; in our church life we have avoided you; and in our personal lives we have shut our hearts to you. Forgive us, restore us, and grant us newness of life through Jesus Christ our Lord. *Amen.*

46. Gracious Father, whose mercy is higher than the heavens, wider than our wanderings and deeper than all sin; receive back to yourself your bewildered and broken children. Forgive our folly and excess, our coldness to human sorrows, our envy of those who prosper and are at ease, our passion for the things of the moment that perish in the grasping, our indifference to those treasures of the spirit which are life and peace, our neglect of wise and gracious laws; and so change our hearts and turn all our desires to yourself that we may love that which you approve, and do that which you command, and with strength and resolution walk in uprightness and charity, to the serving of our brethren, and the glory of your name; through Jesus Christ our Lord. *Amen.*

47. Almighty God, our Father, you have created us for life together: we confess that we have turned from your will. We have not loved each other as you have commanded. We have been quick to claim our own rights and careless of the rights of others. We have taken much and given little. Forgive our disobedience, O God, and strengthen us in love that we may serve you as a faithful people and live together in peace; through Jesus Christ our Lord. *Amen.*

48. Our Creator and Redeemer, we turn to you acknowledging that our pride is greater than our ability, and our faults greater than our virtues. In the days of our prosperity we have forgotten you. We have seated ourselves on the bench of judgment failing to recognize that we are not the ones who are worthy to judge, rather we are the ones who stand at the bar of judgment seeking your mercy and longing for your grace. When you spoke to us, through the needs of our neighbors, we did not hear you for the clamor of our own voices raised in confusing competition with one another. In our folly we have turned from you, from our neighbor, and from the works of your creation. Forgive us. Renew our faltering trust and increase our love through him who trusted us and loved us, even unto death. We rejoice in the assurance of your pardon, and pledge ourselves afresh to you and one another, through Jesus Christ our Lord. *Amen.*

49. Father Eternal, you are readier to forgive our sins than we are to admit them. We have allowed our pride to blind us so that we have not seen the splendor of your handiwork or the wonders of your grace. We have been bold in our profession of loving truth, but by our indifference to its costly demand we have supported hypocrisy. We have talked about loving our neighbor, but we have passed him by when he needed our love. We have said, "Lord, Lord" with our lips and then ignored your commands. Renew your likeness within us and unite us as your family on earth: through him who intercedes for all men, even Jesus Christ our Lord. *Amen.*

50. Gracious Father, we know that all our failures and shortcomings stand revealed in the clear light of your goodness. Forgive our hardness of heart and our smallness of mind; our self-centeredness and our indifference to the agony of others. Forgive our readiness to prejudge the actions of our brethren without taking the time to understand the experiences they have endured. Forgive us for pretending to be in the light when our deeds declare that we have chosen to walk in the way of darkness;

> *Minister:* Lord, have mercy upon us.
> *People:*   Christ, have mercy upon us.
> *Minister:* Lord, have mercy upon us.
> *People:*   *Amen.*

51. Almighty God, Father of our Lord Jesus Christ, we humbly acknowledge our offenses against you by thought and deed. We have neglected opportunities of good which you in your love gave to us. We have been overcome by temptations from which you were ready to guard us. We have looked to men, and not to you, in doing our daily work. We have thought too little of others and too much of our own pleasure in all our plans. But you are ever merciful and gracious to those who turn to you. So now we come to you, beseeching you that you will not cast us out, but will have mercy upon us. Forgive, O Lord, our transgressions, and grant us grace to live hereafter more worthily of our Christian calling, for the glory of your great name. *Amen.*

52. O God, our Creator and Father, you have shown us the light of your glory shining on the face of your Son, Jesus. Let not this light be for our judgment, but

for our liberation, and for our increasing knowledge of yourself. Too often we have found that light too disturbing in its revealing brightness, and we turned from it into darkness and the works of darkness. Forgive us for not following in the way of light; through Jesus Christ our Lord. *Amen.*

53. A broken and contrite heart is something you do not despise, O Father Eternal. We turn to you for help because the burden of the world's suffering is too heavy for us to bear alone, and so is the burden of our guilt: for in ways known and unknown to us we have made our original contribution to mankind's agony. Cast our sins into the sea of your loving forgetfulness, and assure us that in partnership with yourself and with all honest people we may work for that which is good and creative, without fear, through Jesus our Lord and elder Brother. *Amen.*

54. Holy and Righteous Father, we confess our faltering faith, our failures in living, our lost opportunities and untimely efforts, through which we multiply our own distresses.

In mercy bring these things to our remembrance, and then cast them into the sea of your forgetfulness.

Lord of all grace, who in tender love for mankind stretched out your arms upon the Cross. Let not your mercy be far from those who confess their offenses; but cleanse our hearts, pardon and take away our sins; that freed from iniquity, we may evermore cleave to you for your Name's sake. *Amen.*

55. Almighty God, we bow down before you, acknowledging our unworthiness and our sin. You sent

your Son to show us the way of life; yet we have strayed from it continually. You have manifested his kingly right, and we have seen his glory; yet, while offering him the homage of our lips, we have not given him the loyalty of our lives. We have followed our own pleasures; we have sought our own ends; we have lived in selfishness; we have refused the way of the Cross. Have mercy upon us; rebuke our waywardness and folly, and grant us true repentance, that our sins may be forgiven; through Jesus Christ our Lord. *Amen.*

56. We rejoice in the power of your love which overcame the power of death and raised your son from the grave. We confess that we have forgotten the promise of life that the resurrection revealed; for, by forgetting we have allowed ourselves to be defeated by the power of death and despair. Help us once again to turn to you in trust that we may receive the gift of new life, the strength to follow you, and the love to serve you: through Jesus Christ our Lord. *Amen.*

57. Holy God and loving Father, we deplore the coldness of our love, the feebleness of our faith, the poverty of our service.
Forgive us, and free us from the chains of our past transgressions; set us free to serve you with willing mind and undivided heart; through Jesus Christ our Lord. *Amen.*

58. Eternal Father we confess that we have not allowed Jesus Christ to reign at the center of our lives. As a consequence, we have experienced the meaninglessness of chaos, and the loneliness of separation. We

have over-indulged our egos and allowed them to control our thoughts and our tempers. We admit there have been times when we've been unfit to live with. Forgive us for our stupidity and turn us to him, who is the Lord of life, that we may obey him and experience his joy for the benefit, not only of ourselves, but of those in our neighborhood. Help us so to order our lives that we may help resolve the conflicts of our times; through Jesus Christ our Lord. *Amen.*

59. Father, we have sinned. We have relegated you to second place in our lives, and worshipped the power of might, of privilege, and of prejudice; the power of death, the power of bigness, of money, and of national security; the power of intellect, of education, and of sheer numbers. Therefore we repent and turn to you as Lord of all life; Lord of all men and nations; Lord of all people. Forgive us, heal us, help us, and restore us to fellowship with your Son and each other. *Amen.*

60. We come to you, O God our Father, with hearts troubled by the memory and the burden of our offenses: of that which we ought to have done, but have not done; of that which we ought to have spoken, but have not spoken. Of these things, and of all our sins remembered and forgotten, we repent and turn to you. Graciously forgive us; purify and strengthen our hearts; that we may walk steadfastly and uprightly before you all our days, in the love and service of Jesus Christ our Lord. *Amen.*

61. O God of love and mercy, we confess that we have done that which is wrong in your sight. We have

wronged ourselves by yielding to the desires of our lower nature. We have wronged others by word and deed. We have wronged you, O God, for we have failed to be true to the insights you have given us. We have kept our eyes downcast, when you have bidden us to look upward. We have turned our faces away from injustices and evil, when you have called us to encounter the reality of sin and to overcome it. We have hidden behind cliches and slogans instead of searching for the truth. Cleanse our hearts that we may love you above all else and our neighbor as ourselves, through Jesus Christ our Lord. *Amen.*

ASSURANCES OF PARDON

62. Put on then, as God's chosen ones, holy and
beloved, compassion, kindness, lowliness, meekness,
and patience, forbearing one another and, if one has a
complaint against another, forgiving each other; as the
Lord has forgiven you, so you also must forgive.

(Colossians 3:12, 13)

63. Who is a God like thee, pardoning iniquity
and passing over transgression
for the remnant of his inheritance?
He does not retain his anger for ever
because he delights in steadfast love.
He will again have compassion upon us,
he will tread our iniquities under foot.
Thou wilt cast all our sins
into the depths of the sea. *(Micah 7:18, 19)*

64. Let the wicked forsake his way,
and the unrighteous man his thoughts;
let him return to the Lord, that he may have mercy on
him,
and to our God, for he will abundantly pardon.

(Isaiah 55:7)

65. For thus says the high and lofty One
who inhabits eternity, whose name is Holy:
"I dwell in the high and holy place,

and also with him who is of a contrite and humble
    spirit,
to revive the spirit of the humble,
    and to revive the heart of the contrite."

(Isaiah 57:15)

ADVENT

66. The prophet of the Most High . . . will go before
the Lord to prepare his ways, to give knowledge of
salvation to his people in the forgiveness of their sins,
through the tender mercy of our God.

(Luke 1:76-78)

CHRISTMAS

67. [God] chose us in [Christ] before the foundation
of the world, that we should be holy and blameless
before him. He destined us in love to be his sons
through Jesus Christ. . . . In him we have redemption
through his blood, the forgiveness of our trespasses.

(Ephesians 1:4-7)

THE NEW YEAR

68. If any one is in Christ, he is a new creation; the
old has passed away, behold, the new has come. All this
is from God, who through Christ reconciled us to
himself and gave us the ministry of reconciliation; that
is, in Christ God was reconciling the world to himself,
not counting their trespasses against them, and en-
trusting to us the message of reconciliation.

(II Corinthians 5:17, 18, 19)

LENT

69. God shows his love for us in that while we were
yet sinners Christ died for us. Since, therefore, we are

now justified by his blood, much more shall we be saved by him from the wrath of God.

(Romans 5:8, 9)

EASTER

70. We bring you the good news that what God promised to the fathers, this he has fulfilled to us their children by raising Jesus. . . . Let it be known to you therefore, brethren, that through this man forgiveness of sins is proclaimed to you, and by him every one that believes is freed from everything from which you could not be freed by the law of Moses.

(Acts 13:32, 33, 38, 39)

PRAYERS FOR THE SEASONS
OF THE CHURCH YEAR

ADVENT

71. Almighty God, give us grace in this our present life, which your Son Jesus Christ in great humility came to share, that being armed with the light of your truth and love we may overcome the darkness of evil; so that in the final triumph of your Kingdom we may share in life eternal; through him who lives and rules with you and the Holy Spirit now and forever. *Amen*.

72. Blessed Lord, through whose gift of the Holy Scriptures we learn of your mighty saving acts for mankind, help us so to hear, remember, and understand your Holy Word, that strengthened and sustained thereby, we may know in this temporal life the hope of eternity which you have given us in our Savior Jesus Christ, who lives and rules with you and the Holy Spirit now and ever. *Amen*.

73. O Sun of Righteousness, promised of the prophet; pierce with the pure light of your presence the shadows of strife and evil that envelop mankind. Come with healing. Awaken us from the trance of self-centeredness. Cleanse and quicken us during these days of preparation so that on the Holy Night of Christ's birth we may join our voices with those of the angel host, singing "Glory" and "Peace." *Amen*.

CHRISTMAS

74. Jesus, begotten of the Father, born of Mary; make this holy season a reminder to us that as you once entered the realm of time and space, so now you enter our earthly existence. Let the joy of your presence inspire our Christmas joy, our hymns of praise, our prayers of thanksgiving. *Amen.*

75. O God, you have illumined this holy night with the light that is in Jesus Christ. May that Light, whose mystery we have glimpsed in our present life, guide us also to the ultimate joy of eternal life, for the sake of Jesus Christ who lives and rules with you and the Holy Spirit now and ever. *Amen.*

76. O God, who in the birth of your Holy Child, Jesus, have visited and redeemed your people, grant that he may be born in us so that we may share his joy and peace, and be strengthened to worship and serve you acceptably through him, our Lord and Savior Jesus Christ. *Amen.*

77. O God of pity, hear us as we remember those for whom the joy of this day is shadowed; the poor, the lonely, the unloved, and those who have no helper. Let those who know your love abound in sympathy and kindness, that, having freely received, they may also freely give. Remember in your mercy the infirm and the aged, the sick and the sad, the heavy-laden and all who mourn. According to their several necessities and wants, reveal yourself to them in help; through Jesus Christ our Redeemer. *Amen.*

78. God our Father, we thank you that you have caused your light to shine in darkness, your glory to be revealed where it is least expected, and that this continues to be your way. We give you thanks for the fullness of your grace in Jesus our Savior. We thank you for the humble shepherds and the loving Mother, and for all that light breaking through into our darkness. Glory be to you, O God most high. *Amen.*

EPIPHANY

79. O God, who by a star led gentiles to your Son, mercifully lead us, who know you now by faith, to see the beauty of your eternal greatness, through the same Jesus Christ, our Lord, who lives and rules with you and the Holy Spirit now and ever. *Amen.*

80. O God, the light of whose countenance continues to flood the world; although we have no star in the heavens to guide us as did those ancient magi, we are grateful that you illumine our perilous journey and keep us on a steady course through life. Give us courage to go on and faith to endure. Grant that whatever may occur during our earthly quest we may not lose confidence, so that in the end we may share the title "wise" with those who sought you at your Son's Epiphany. *Amen.*

THE TRANSFIGURATION

81. O God, who in the glorious transfiguration of your only Son and in the witness of the Patriarchs confirmed the mystery of your redemptive love, and who in your Son called us also to be sons; give us therefore a share in the work and glory of his eternal

Kingdom, who lives and rules with you and the Holy
Spirit now and ever. *Amen.*

LENT AND HOLY WEEK

82. Lord Christ, since for our sakes you were content
to bear sorrow, want, and death; grant to us such a
measure of your Spirit that we may follow you in all
your courage and self-denial; and help us by your great
love to aid the afflicted, to relieve the needy and the
destitute, to share the burdens of the heavy-laden, and
to see you in all who are poor and desolate; for you live
and reign with the Father and the Holy Spirit, one God,
now and for evermore. *Amen.*

83. O God, our Father, as on Palm Sunday the
crowds welcomed our Savior by casting their garments
before his feet; enable us in this hour to cast our
garments of pride before him, that in the spirit of
humility every knee shall bow and every tongue confess
that Jesus Christ is Lord, to your eternal glory. *Amen.*

84. Blessed Lord Jesus; as once the multitude
welcomed you with shouts and the waving of palm
branches, we too, on this anniversary of your triumphant entry into Jerusalem, welcome you into our lives.
Keep us from Jerusalem's sins: the sins of rejection,
betrayal, and crucifixion. Help us to be faithful, but
forgive us if we fail. *Amen.*

85. O God, in the Sacrament of Holy Communion
you have given us a memorial of the Passion of your
Son; help us to receive this Communion of his Body and
Blood in such a way that we may see in our lives the

44

fruits of your redemption, through Jesus Christ our Lord. *Amen*.

86. O Lord Jesus Christ, our Savior, we thank you for bearing our griefs and carrying our sorrows. Draw us closer to the cross that we may be drawn closer to you and to one another, and we shall praise you together with the Father and the Holy Spirit, world without end. *Amen*.

EASTER

87. O God, as your Son our Risen Lord made himself known to his disciples in the breaking of bread, give us eyes of faith that we may recognize his living presence with us; and that, guided and strengthened by him, we may do your work in the world; through Jesus Christ who lives and rules with you and the Holy Spirit now and ever. *Amen*.

88. O God, help us, who have celebrated the victory of our Lord's resurrection to experience the death of our evil ways and to share in his eternal life, who lives and rules with you and the Holy Spirit now and ever. *Amen*.

ASCENSION

89. King of glory, Lord of interstellar space and Conqueror of time; your Ascension frees you from the limits of earthly existence and makes you available to the whole cosmos, and to all peoples. For this we worship and adore you now and forever. *Amen*.

90. O God, glorious King, who by the resurrection and ascension of our Lord Jesus Christ opened your

Kingdom to all who believe, do not abandon us to our own weakness, we beg of you, but send your Holy Spirit to strengthen us and to lead us on to truth and peace; through Jesus Christ, who lives and rules with you and the Holy Spirit, now and ever. *Amen.*

PENTECOST

91. O God, as in the past you sent your Holy Spirit to enlighten and instruct your faithful people, so now by the same Spirit help us to make right decisions and to enjoy his reassuring presence; through Jesus Christ, who lives and rules with you and the Holy Spirit, now and ever. *Amen.*

92. Grant, O Lord, that we may experience our own Day of Pentecost, when worshipping you with one heart we shall be empowered to speak your word of truth in the meeting places of men, so that all may hear in the language they can understand. Teach us to put our knowledge into meaningful action, and to love the world and people even as you love us. Be with us in all the events of life that we may have light for our darkness, and joy in your service; through Jesus Christ our Lord, to whom with you, O Father, and the Holy Spirit, be all praise and glory. *Amen.*

TRINITY SUNDAY

93. Eternal God, who in creative power, redemptive love, and abiding presence disclosed yourself to us as the Glorious Trinity and yet as the One True God to whom alone our worship is due, keep us faithful in your service and defend us in the midst of the hostilities of this world; through Jesus Christ; who lives and rules with you and the Holy Spirit, now and ever. *Amen.*

THE REFORMATION

94. Almighty God, who by the words of your prophets in every age have sought to reform and renew your people; open our ears to hear your words, that we, being truly renewed and reformed, may joyfully live and proclaim your Gospel in our day; through Jesus Christ our Lord. *Amen.*

A DAY OF GENERAL OR SPECIAL THANKSGIVING

95. Almighty God and loving Father, you have again fulfilled your promise, that while the earth remains, seedtime and harvest shall not fail. You have given to us the fruits of the earth in their season, and you have crowned the year with your goodness. Accept now, in your endless mercy, our sacrifice of praise and thanksgiving, and grant us grace to share with others that which you have given us in such abundance; through Jesus Christ our Lord. *Amen.*

96. Generous God, who in creation provided enough for all mankind, forgive us for the selfishness which claims too much and gives too little; and make us grateful for him who, though he was rich, became poor for our sakes, even Jesus Christ our Lord. *Amen.*

97. Gracious God, you have provided all things for our need; accept the thanks of your people for your generous gifts and for your steadfast love, in the name of your greatest gift, Jesus Christ our Lord. *Amen.*

98. Our Father and our Friend, we thank you for the promise of Jesus—"I have called you friends"—and for his unfailing friendship, and for all the friends we have

made in the fellowship of your church where we are no longer strangers, through the love of Jesus Christ. *Amen.*

99. Almighty and most merciful Father, the giver of every good and perfect gift, we give you thanks for all the opportunities of our life and for the promise of eternal life, for your love as our Father, for the example of our Savior, for the enabling power of your Spirit, and for the church as our spiritual home, through the head of the church, Jesus Christ our Lord. *Amen.*

100. We give thanks to you, O God, for the generosity of your grace; for the gift of Christ, who took our nature and understands our problems; who gives us the strength to overcome our temptations; whose cross empowers us to bear our sufferings; and whose resurrection enables us to overcome the fear of death; through the same Jesus Christ our Lord. *Amen.*

101. O God, you called us to be pilgrims of hope; we thank you for all whom you have given to be near and dear to us; for fellow members of the household of faith, for friends and family, for comrades and co-workers, for pastors and teachers and for all with whom we are linked in the service of Jesus Christ our Lord. *Amen.*

102. O God our Father, we thank you for the wonder of our calling in Christ, for the joy that comes from his service, for our faith in the victory of his kingdom, and for the hope of life everlasting, through Jesus Christ our Lord. *Amen.*

103. Almighty God and gracious giver, we thank you for the gospel which called us out of darkness into your marvelous light; for the grace that enables us to become more than conquerors through him that loved us; and for the assurance that neither death nor life shall be able to separate us from your love in Jesus Christ our Lord. *Amen.*

104. Almighty God on this day of national thanksgiving, we thank you for the goodly heritage of our nation. We rejoice in the richness of our countrysides and the wealth of our resources. We thank you for the ideals of faith and freedom upon which our nation was founded. We remember with gratitude those who have sacrificed of themselves to maintain these ideals in honor and fidelity. Forgive us, we pray, our sins of injustice and apathy, of racial alienation and social pride. Spare us from the sin of ingratitude and lift us to noble living, that we may use our prosperity for generosity, our power with responsibility, and our liberty for self-discipline and good works. Bind all the peoples of our nation together in unity of purpose and devotion, that we may serve each other in Christian love and lead the nations of the world in the search for lasting peace and brotherhood, through Christ, the Prince of Peace. *Amen.*

105. O Lord, there is so much to thank you for.

Day by day we have more than enough to eat. We can pick and choose, and eat what we like. We're comfortably housed and clothed. We have all that we need and more. We thank you for these and other blessings which satisfy our physical needs.

Increase our sense of thankfulness to remember
those who are homeless:
those who are exiled;
those who are orphaned;
those who are naked;
those who are oppressed;
those who are diseased by malnutrition and illnesses;
those who are starving;
those who are dying;
those who are our sisters and brothers.
There seems at times so little we may do to help them
in a practical way.

Barriers of bureaucracy divide us. Apathy makes us
impotent. Move among us in the power of your Spirit
that we may dare to move mountains, and try the
impossible, because we are your people caring for your
people. *Amen.*

106. God of our fathers: we praise you for all your
servants who, having witnessed to you on earth, now
live with you in heaven. Keep us in fellowship with
them until we meet with all the faithful in the joy of
your kingdom, through Jesus Christ our Lord. *Amen.*

LITANIES OF THANKSGIVING
AND INTERCESSION

107.

Minister: Thanks be to you, most glorious God, for the revelation of yourself to our poor world, and for your commission to your Church to proclaim the Gospel of Christ to every creature;

People: Thanks be to you, O God.

Minister: For the early disciples who were sent forth by Christ to proclaim the coming of the kingdom; for the apostles of his Word who carried the Gospel through the Roman Empire and to the world beyond; for those who brought the Gospel to this land;

People: We praise you, O God.

Minister: For all those who, in the ages of darkness, kept alive the light, and who while all slumbered and slept, were faithful to their Lord's command; for all who in our times have recalled the Church to her task of loving the world; for those who have gone to the troubled, distressed and sorrowful places of men with the joyful news, and have sought out the dark places of earth to bring light to them that dwell in the shadow of death.

People: We praise you, O God.

Minister: For all of your servants who have made the final witness, that of martyrdom;

People: We praise you, O God.

Minister: We remember, O Father, that your Son died with his arms outstretched to embrace the world;

People: Therefore, help us to witness compassionately to the truth of your love wherever people work, or gather together.

Minister: You are the light of the world.

People: A city that is set on a hill cannot be hid.

Minister: Let your light so shine before mankind, that they may see your good works,

People: And glorify our Father who is in heaven. *Amen.*

108.

Minister: We thank you, O Father, for the wonders of your grace:

People: For never leaving nor forgetting us.

Minister: We thank you for continuing to love this world although it continues to ignore you:

People: For sending your Son in the fulfillment of time to obey your commandment of love.

Minister: We thank you for redeeming our times;

People: For sanctifying the everyday events of life with your presence.

Minister: We thank you for showing us the way we ought to live,

People: For setting before us an end which defiant men may not destroy.

Minister: Renew your likeness within us.

People: Enable us to work with you as patient laborers in your work of reconciliation.

Minister: We rejoice in the gifts of Christ our Lord

People: And in the hope they bring to the whole world.

Minister: The gift of love

People: The gift of peace,

Minister: The gift of trust.

People: Help us to accept them humbly, O Father, and to use them for your glory in our homes, and fellowships, and businesses.

Minister: Teach us by our repentance to wait upon you in the patience of faith, the expectancy of hope, and the excitement of love.

People: *Amen.*

109.

Minister: As you surprised the world by joy in the eventful act of the Word become flesh,

People: We pause to reflect in wonder upon the beauty of your gracious ways.

Minister: We pray that we may learn increasingly not to be defeated by the bad news of the world, but instead, to rejoice in the Good News of your love for us.

People: Make us ever sensitive, O Father, to the high demands of your way of life.

Minister: By their faithfulness to the Good News may the community of faith guide this nation into the ways of peace, truth, and life.

People: And may our prayers be answered in the quality of our lives lived for you and our neighbor.

Minister: Teach the President of this country, and all who are in government, by the word of your wisdom, that your Name may be honored in our days.

People: And that our country may be blessed with the works of your Spirit, honesty, joy, trust, and compassion.

Minister: Hear us, O Father, in the fellowship of prayer:

People: For we know that you will withhold no good thing from those who ask you.

Minister: We praise you, and glorify you in the wonder of your ways.

People: Amen.

110.

Minister: For the beauty we are privileged to see.

People: We thank you, O Father.

Minister: For the consciousness which characterizes the uniqueness of our creation.

People: We thank you, O Father.

Minister: For the light of your revelation shining on the face of Jesus the Christ.

People: We thank you, O Father.

Minister: For your people in every country that they may shine as lights in a dark world:

People: Lord, hear our prayer.

Minister: For all the works of merciful people that they may bring new understanding to others:

People: Lord, hear our prayer.

Minister: For those who are ill, especially for those who know the dark shadows of the valley of death, that the light of your presence may heal and comfort them:

People: Lord, hear our prayer.

Minister: For lands and their people darkened by the anger of war, that the light of your peace may shine upon them:

People: Lord, hear our prayer. *Amen.*

111.

Minister: Eternal Father, you have given us knowledge of yourself through the faithful ministry of your Son. Help us by faith to join the ranks of Christ's disciples, and to learn from Him at first hand.

People: Help us so to do, O Lord.

Minister: We remember with thankfulness our Lord's love of life, His identity with the ordinary folk, His joy in good companionship, and His delight in the beauty and grandeur of your world.

People: Increase our joy, O Lord.

Minister: We remember how he used His freedom to do your will regardless of the consequences; of how He chose the way of sacrificial love rather than the way of personal convenience and moral compromise; and of how He used His power by not using it.

People: Increase our love, O Lord.

Minister: We remember how His faithfulness to you led Him from Galilee to Jerusalem, and from Jerusalem to the Cross, where He died for us sinners.

People: Increase our loyalty to you, O Lord.

Minister: We remember that you did not desert your Son on the Cross, nor leave Him to the triumph of the tomb; but that you raised Him in glory and victory on the eighth day of creation, the New Day of the Lord.

People: Increase our strength, O Lord.

Minister: Help us never to be forgetful of the great things you have accomplished through the work of your Son, and to follow Him with joy wherever He may lead us.

People: Increase our faith, O Lord.

Minister: Our time is one of despair and expectation, despair because of our inability to save ourselves, of expectation because of our hope that you will raise up for yourself, out of the wilderness of our complacency, a loyal and victorious people.

People: Increase our hope, O Lord.

Minister: Redeem our times, O Father, and guide us in the way of righteousness, truth, peace, faith, hope, and love.

People: Increase our desire to serve you, O Lord.

Minister: You are our God, and we are your people, therefore help us to be faithful to you at all times, and to triumph over all evil in the power of the Holy Spirit.

People: And to your Name be the praise and the glory, for ever, and ever. *Amen.*

PRAYERS FOR ILLUMINATION

112. Holy Spirit, purify us that our ears may be unplugged and that we may respond to you in love and joy, ready to do your work, to share in the fellowship of your people, and to bear the Cross with those who lay down their lives for your glory. *Amen.*

113. Let your Word come upon us with clarity, O God, that we may know your Holy Will, and write it in our hearts with the power of the Spirit that we may have the strength to do and to bear the same, through Jesus Christ our Lord. *Amen.*

114. O God, the Father of Lights, in whom there is no darkness at all, dispel the darkness of our ignorance and unbelief by the radiance of your Word, through Jesus Christ the Light of the World. *Amen.*

115. O Lord Jesus, let not your Word become a judgment upon us, that we hear it and do it not, that we know it and love it not, that we believe it and obey it not. We ask this of you who live eternally with the Father and the Holy Spirit, world without end. *Amen.*

116. O Merciful God, always ready to reveal yourself to the children of men, give us eyes to see, ears to hear, and hearts to understand your Word. And help us to retain your truth that we may obey your law all the days of our life. Through Jesus Christ our Lord. *Amen.*

117. Let your Gospel, O Lord, come to us, not in word only, but also in power, and in the Holy Spirit, and in much assurance; that, with humble, teachable, and obedient hearts, we may receive what you have revealed and do always that which you have commanded; through Jesus Christ our Lord. *Amen.*

118. O Lord our God, since you have given your Word to be a lamp to our feet and a light to our path; grant us grace to receive your truth in faith and love, that by it we may be prepared for every good word and work, to the glory of your Name; through Jesus Christ our Lord. *Amen.*

119. O God, whose Word is a lamp for our feet, guide us by the beams of your gospel that we may become the children of light and the heirs of everlasting day, through Jesus Christ the Sun of Righteousness. *Amen.*

120. Our God, who has taught us your way through the obedience of prophets, evangelists and saints, missionaries and martyrs, keep us in that way by the illumination of the Holy Spirit and the love of Jesus Christ our Lord. *Amen.*

121. Gracious Father, since faith comes by hearing your Word, help us to listen to the scriptures with all attention, that they may criticize our faults, confirm our faith, and console our spirits, through Jesus Christ the Word made flesh. *Amen.*

122. Eternal God, give us devout hearts to cling to your promises in Holy Scripture that we may be edified through the power of the Holy Sprit. *Amen.*

123. Holy and loving Father, grant that your children may joyfully listen to the reading and preaching of your Word, so that they may unite faith with wisdom, and godly virtue with true gratitude, through Jesus Christ our Lord. *Amen.*

124. Almighty, ever-gracious Father, forasmuch as all our salvation depends upon our having truly understood your holy Word, therefore grant us that our hearts be set free from worldly things so that we may with all diligence and faith hear and apprehend your holy Word, that we may thereby understand your gracious will and in all sincerity live according to the same, to your praise and glory, through our Lord Jesus Christ. *Amen.*

BIDDING PRAYERS

Let us pray for our country:

125. Once again, O heavenly Father, we are reminded of our failure as a nation to be a faithful steward of the treasures granted to us out of the storehouse of your grace. Let us not be defeated by the constant evidence of our failures, but grant us a vision of our land, fair as we might be; a land of justice, where care should be taken for the needs of all; a land of brotherhood, where success should be founded on service, and honor should be given to worth alone; a land of peace, where order should not rest on force, but on the respect of citizens for one another. Hear the silent prayers of our hearts as we pledge our time, strength, and thought to hasten the day of your righteousness. *Amen.*

Let us pray for the communities of learning:

126. You have inspired us to seek for truth, to desire perfection, and to rejoice in beauty. Grant, therefore, that we may never allow our colleges and universities to become mechanistic processes and systems devoid of enthusiasm, inspiration, and humanity. As you have blessed our schools, colleges and universities with a great heritage of learning and wisdom so may we, who are their inheritors, transform them into reconciling forces in the world through dedication to humanity. Make us willing to be wrong for the sake of your truth, and willing to be despised for the sake of your glory.

Help us to lead others in the paths of your righteousness rather than following the ways of expediency and cynicism; through Jesus Christ our Lord. *Amen.*

Let us pray for the community of faith:

127. You have taught us that men shall not live by bread alone, but by your Word, which is the bread of life. Grant that those who dare to trust in you may be liberated from the control of convenient customs to serve you honestly and bravely in the days of their earthly existence. Use this occasion, we pray, that those who have been deaf may hear, and that those who have been blind may see. Teach us, once again, what is good. And strengthen us by our life together to do justice, to love mercy, and to live in fellowship with you, our God. *Amen.*

Let us pray for those who mourn:

128. We remember before you all whose hearts are troubled by the separation of death. Comfort them in their agony, and grant them peace for their anxiety. Thus do we pray for the families and friends of _____, for those who have lost their dearest ones in battle, or in the civil conflicts of our time. *Amen.*

Let us pray for the Communion of Saints:

129. We thank you for the good witness and faithful lives of all those who have served you by serving their fellows in politics, medicine, education, social action, civil service, and in every walk of life. Keep them in your continuous fellowship and prosper the work they have done. Take away the veils from each heart, and join us in one communion with your servants who have trusted you, and were not ashamed.

Grant that at the last all that is good in us may prevail over what is evil: that everything may be brought into harmony with your will, and that you may be all in all. *Amen.*

Let us remember how Jesus was betrayed, and given up into the hands of wicked men:

130. Lord Jesus, we remember today that it was one of your own familiar friends who betrayed you, and we know that there is nothing which so breaks the heart as the disloyalty of one called "friend." Grant that we may not betray you.

Save us,
  From the cowardice,
    which would disown you when it is hard to be true
      to you;
  From the disloyalty,
    which betrays you in the hour when you need
      someone to stand by you;
  From the fickleness,
    which blows hot and cold in its devotion;
  From the fair-weather friendship,
    which, when things are difficult or dangerous,
      makes us ashamed to show whose we are and
      whom we serve.

Let us remember how Jesus suffered death upon the Cross:

Lord Jesus, help us to remember
  The lengths to which your love was ready to go;
  That having loved your own you loved them to the
    very end;
  That you gave the love which cannot be surpassed,
    the love which lays down its life for its friends;

That it was while men were yet enemies that you died
    for them.
Let us remember how Jesus now lives and reigns:
Help us to remember
    That the Crucified Lord is the Risen Lord;
    That the Cross has become the Crown;
So grant unto us,
    To trust in his love;
    To live in his presence;
    That we may share in his glory.
This we ask for the sake of your love, O God. *Amen.*

Let us remember God in Creation:
131. O God, Our Father, we thank you for your
creating power:
    That you have made all things and made them well;
    That you have given us all things richly to enjoy;
    For the beauty and the bounty of this fair earth;
    And for the life which can make all things new:
    We thank you, O Father.
    Forgive us if in pride, in selfishness, and in anger we
    have misused your gifts, and have used for death that
    which was meant for life.
Let us remember God in Redemption:
O Lord Jesus Christ, the Son, we thank you for your
redeeming power:
    That you loved us and gave yourself for us;
    That you gave your life a ransom for us and for many;
    That you were obedient unto death, even the death of
        the Cross:
    We thank you, O Christ.
    Forgive us if we have treated your love lightly, like a

63

little thing, and if we have never even begun to love
you

as you have first loved us.

Let us remember God in Providence:

O Holy Spirit of God, we thank you for your
sustaining power:

For the guidance you have given us;

For the knowledge you have brought to us;

For your continually upholding, strengthening, pro-
tecting power:

We thank you, O Spirit of God.

Forgive us if we have tried to live life alone, or have
despoiled

ourselves of the divine help we might have had from
you. *Amen.*

For those in authority:

Let us pray for those in authority over us;

The president of our nation, and his cabinet;

Members of the Congress of the United States;

Judges of the Supreme Court;

The governor of the State of ———, and members of
our state legislature;

Those in positions of civic trust in the Town of ———;

And all others in authority.

132. Lord, give to all these people who have
authority over others,

the wisdom to govern well,

And the grace to know in their hearts

That nothing is firm that is not just, and that the test of
justice

is to turn people from following after evil,
To seek what is good.

For those in trouble:
Let us pray for those in trouble: the sick; the bereaved;
the lonely; those without work; all victims of men's
injustice; those who doubt the goodness of men or of
God; and those exposed to danger by their obedience to
God's will.

133. Lord Jesus, pioneer of our salvation,
Who were yourself made perfect through suffering,
and have taught us that in relieving the suffering of
    others
We minister to you,
And in patiently enduring our own
We may follow you;
Bless all those in trouble.
Help us, with love and wisdom to serve them,
And so remain one with suffering humanity
For whom you were willing to endure a criminal's
    death,
in order to open to us all the way of life eternal. *Amen.*

134. O Savior Christ, Son of Man and Son of God,
Who have yourself passed through the test of suffering
    and so are able to help those meeting their test now;
Arm all who this day meet temptation
    with an unashamed reliance on your power,
    and an unshakeable faith in your goodness,
That having endured with you the heat of the battle,
They may with you share the glory of victory. *Amen.*

135. Lord Jesus, ruler of all nature,
You have the power and authority
to cast out all that is evil,
And yet you patiently endured temptation and pain
To open to us the Kingdom of God;
Be with all who suffer,
And help your church,
To which you have given authority over the spirits of
   evil,
So to minister to those in trouble
That the bitterness may be drained from their suffering,
And they may find you with them in trouble,
And themselves sharing with you the burden of the
   world's redemption. *Amen.*

PRAYERS FOR SPECIAL OCCASIONS AND SPECIAL GRACES

AT THE INSTALLATION OF A PASTOR

136. Almighty and everlasting God; Since you have established your holy church for faith, for worship, and for fellowship, mercifully hear our prayer for this congregation (parish). Grant to it all things needful for its spiritual and temporal welfare. Strengthen the faithful, encourage the sick, comfort those who mourn, grant peace to the aged, arouse the indifferent and careless, recover the fallen, forgive the penitent. Remove from the hearts of those who call themselves your children all hindrances that may keep them from loving and serving you fully. Teach your people to give in proportion to what they have received in order that our vision for the future may become a present reality. We pray for him who today begins his ministry in this congregation. Grant him the direction, aid and counsel of your Holy Spirit:

That he may serve you with a pure heart and a holy life,
That he may preach your Word with power,
That he may faithfully administer your sacraments,
That in all things he may be a good and faithful steward of the divine mysteries.

And so we give ourselves to you, pastor and people, bodies and souls. Use us for the upbuilding of your kingdom and to the honor and glory of your ever blessed Name. *Amen.*

137. O God, in every age you have called your children to walk in the way of truth and life and have revealed this way supremely in Jesus Christ. Bless now, we pray, this servant who has dared to offer himself to your service in this place and among these people. Grant him the courage not to conform—but without arrogance; the honesty which will enable him to serve you with conviction and integrity—but without self-righteousness; the love by which all life and every human relationship is brought to highest meaning—but without sentimentality. Through the Holy Spirit working in his heart lead and compel him in every familiar way or strange new path in which you beckon him to follow you.

O Jesus Christ, you came as the living Word revealed and enfleshed in the human form which is every man's earthly attire, we pray you to rule the plans and dreams, the hopes and aspirations of this man who has been called to be a minister of this same Word. Keep him mindful both of his frailty as a vessel of the redemptive Word and his unconquerable power as a recipient of your grace. Help him to accept and rejoice in your Lordship over his life, that he may be a faithful and profitable servant. When he is tempted to substitute his own words for your Word, stand with him in all the glory of the truth which is made alive in you. Whenever he would divert his time or energies into ways not in accord with your purpose, direct him on the straight way with singleness of mind and sight. Set before him, we ask, doors of great opportunity and strengthen him that he may open and enter.

O Holy Spirit, source of wisdom and center of all real power in the Church, enter into the life of this your minister. In his moments of doubt, his hours of joy, and his days of loneliness, be present with him. Sustain him; make him bold and full of courage to proclaim the Gospel with might, that men's hearts may be set on fire, their minds swept free of darkness and their spirits filled with love. Never leave him without your comfort. Guide, direct, strengthen him that in every ministry which he undertakes he may seek only to glorify your name among men and serve them according to your will. When he is cast down, lift him up. When he errs, correct him. When he yields to pride or arrogance, humble him. When he misses the mark of his high calling, forgive him and lead him back again.

O God the Father, Son and Holy Spirit, in your great mercy and persistent suffering love, receive this your child and servant into his ministry within the flock which you have gathered here. Open the hearts of those who have covenanted to worship and serve with him, that together these people may enter into all the riches of the Faith, both now and forever. And to you the triune God be all honor, majesty, glory and power now and through every age. *Amen.*

AT A MARRIAGE SERVICE

138. Eternal God, we pray the blessing of your grace upon these your servants, now united in marriage. May they know each other as you know them and give themselves to each other as you have given your self.

When they discover differences between each other,

69

teach them to accept them and find in those very differences their greater joy and love.

When they are anxious about who they are as persons or as husband or wife, may they discover new meaning in their living together.

When they face discouragement and disillusionment, may they have the courage to reveal their inner selves to each other until they call forth from each other's person that which is real and true. May they discover and rediscover the person in each other.

Save them from pretense, from unrelieved hostilities and unspoken regrets, from self-centeredness and selfishness and from the disabling effects of broken communication.

Make every moment of estrangement lead to reunion. Mend and heal all brokenness and loneliness. Enable them to turn every trouble imposed upon them or originated in them into an opportunity for greater and more mature expression of love and understanding.

To this end, we ask, present before them your own example of victory through hardship, suffering, and the cross, granting them the joys of that victory which comes only through the burdens and problems of life.

Be yourself in their marriage to reveal the overflowing grace of your love, the depth and constancy of true commitment, until their relationship to each other is symbolic of your relationship to us.

We offer these prayers in Jesus' Name and to his Glory. *Amen.*

FOR A COMMUNITY LEADER

139. This moment comes, our Father, and out of the

mixed harvest of our day, we stand before you in grateful recollection. We rejoice in this company of dedicated men and women whose talent of mind and gifts of spirit serve our community.

Especially, our gratitude goes to you for your servant whose service we here recall. For the heritage of faith to which he was born, for the home and church which molded his life, we thank you. For the warmth and honesty which draw friends to him and for the many facets of his spirit which serve our community so well, thanks be to you.

Make us worthy of such leadership; encourage among us men of like devotion; and, in the midst of your bounty of talent and daily sustenance, give us grateful hearts. *Amen.*

FOR HOSPITALS

140. Lord Jesus, who
in the days of your earthly life went about
healing men, women and children
from all kinds of sickness and disease:
be with those who work in our hospitals
to rescue our brothers and sisters
from illness of the body,
and give us all
such a measure of your Good Spirit
that our comings and goings
among our neighbors
may bring soundness of body,
mind and spirit.
This we desire
in thankfulness to you. *Amen.*

FOR THE IMPROVEMENT OF RACE RELATIONS

141. Loving Father, you have made all humanity in your likeness and love all you have made; do not let the world separate itself from you by building barriers of race and color.

As your Son, Our Saviour, was born of a Hebrew mother, yet rejoiced in the faith of a Syrian woman and a Roman soldier, welcomed the Greeks who sought him, and had his cross carried by an African, so teach us rightly to recognize the members of all races as fellow-heirs to your kingdom. We ask this in the name of Christ Jesus, the Prince of Peace. *Amen.*

FOR THE RIGHT USE OF MONEY

142. O God, you have taught us in your Word that the love of money is the root of evil, grant us such an attitude toward money that we may not be deceived by its attractiveness nor deluded by its dangers. Forgive us for the times when we have coveted more of the world's goods than we really need. Increase in us charity for all men that we may with joy use the gifts entrusted to us. Reveal to us as you did to your apostle, Paul, the secret of facing plenty and hunger, abundance and want. Shame our selfishness, and bless our generosity. In the name of him who reminded us how hard it is for a rich man to enter the kingdom of God. *Amen.*

FOR OUR MILITARY MEN

143. Eternal God, we remember before you our sons serving in the military forces of our country, especially those in danger on the field of armed action. Grant them to know that our love goes to them, and that wherever they are, your presence is there. We ask

forgiveness that our inability to preserve the peace has placed them in this danger, and that our world anger at itself erupts so often in war, through Jesus Christ, the Prince of Peace. *Amen.*

FOR THE BLIND

144. Almighty God, we pray your guidance for the blind. Lacking physical sight, may those gathered here find the Light of insight and victory within the mind. Deliver us all from the profounder blindness of the spirit which coarsens, rots, and drains away the joy of life. May those who have found their own peace bring courage and hope to those who have only recently lost their sight. And grant especially the goal of self-help and cooperative victory over the problems that beset the blind. This prayer we ask in the name of Christ our Lord. *Amen.*

FOR OUR NEIGHBORS

145. Gracious God, giving our neighbors to us, and us to them,
and bidding us love our neighbors as ourselves;
help us by loving to understand,
and by understanding to help,
and to have the grace to accept their help,
along the way to your Kingdom;
through Jesus Christ our Lord. *Amen.*

FOR THOSE WHO HELP OTHERS

146. O Lord of life, be with those who visit and work among people who are in need of patience, guidance, and assistance of many kinds; bless them in their work of caring for others; in the name of the Chief Shepherd of us all, Jesus Christ our Lord. *Amen.*

FOR SCHOOLS

147. O Lord Jesus Christ, born on earth
That all people may have life more abundantly;
Give your blessing to our School Board
And to the administrators, teachers and students of our
    schools,
That they may seek with singleness of purpose
What is good and true and beautiful;
That they may more and more gain
A right judgment in all things;
That they may willingly forsake
What is deceptive, degrading, and cheap
In order to gain for themselves
And share with others
Those things that are ennobling, dependable, and of
    great worth;
This we desire
In thankfulness to you. *Amen.*

FOR CHRISTIAN EDUCATORS

148. Almighty God, the fountain of wisdom, power
and love, lead our educators in the wisdom that leads to
humility, with the power that lives to serve, and the love
that unites and recreates all mankind, through Jesus
Christ our greatest Teacher and Lord. *Amen.*

FOR COMPASSION

149. Eternal and ever-present God, remember in
your mercy all those whose road through life is hard
and sometimes made harder by our neglect or closed
minds: the poor who live nearby in rotting, unsafe
buildings; the young men and women whose way to
fulfillment is blocked by the color of their skin and the

74

ignorance or the mindless fears their fellowmen have of them; the innocent victims of war. We remember all of these and more. We ask you to help us find ways to relieve the awful burden of human suffering, and if there is some way we can carry it for a while, show us how; in the name of Jesus Christ our Lord. *Amen.*

FOR THE EXTENSION OF GOD'S KINGDOM

150. Lord, who blessed the work of the Apostle's hands to the spread of the gospel, grant us in our several vocations diligently to labor for the extension of your kingdom; for the sake of him who gave himself for the life of the world, your Son our Savior Jesus Christ. *Amen.*

FOR TRUST

151. Father of mercies, who feeds the birds and clothes the lilies, grant us grace not to be anxious about our needs, but to trust in your love and providence while we seek to do your will on earth as it is done in heaven; through him who is our way, our truth, and our life, even Jesus Christ our Lord. *Amen.*

FOR PEACE

152. O Lord, grant that in our disorder we may never doubt your order, and that in all our hostilities we may always be conscious of your peaceful purposes. Give us a margin of tolerance which will respect others and a degree of self-restraint which will create peace in our hearts, our homes, our communities, and our nations; through Jesus Christ our Lord. *Amen.*

153. O God, you have called the peacemakers your children; grant us your peace which passes all under-

standing, that amid the tensions and strife of our time we may live peaceably with all people. Look in mercy upon the nations of the world and enable them to walk in the way of peace, through him who is the Prince of Peace, Jesus Christ our Lord. *Amen.*

FORGIVENESS

154. Almighty God, we rejoice that you have given us another day and another opportunity of following you, of receiving your forgiveness, and of turning toward our neighbors. For the riches of the forgiveness, we have received, grant us the mercy to forgive even our enemies. This we ask in the name of him who in dying forgave all men, and who by his love embraced them as brothers, even Jesus Christ our Lord. *Amen.*

OBEDIENCE

155. Our Father, who in the beginning spoke through the stillness of the morning, speak above the static of our day. Grant that, in spite of the babble of our confusion, we may hear your voice, and instead of the vain boastings of party, class, and sect, we may heed your command to make straight your way. *Amen.*

GUIDANCE

156. Keep us close to yourself in all we do this day and through the coming week; in our labours strengthen us; in our studies illumine us; in our troubles comfort us; in our comforts trouble us; and in our friendships enrich us. Help us to share in your concern for the world in which we live. Look through our eyes that we may see the heart-hungers, the hurts, and the suffering of your children. Instruct us in the

school of obedience that we may follow him who is our Teacher, our Leader, and our Elder Brother, even Jesus Christ our Lord, to whom with you, O Father, and the Holy Spirit be all honor and glory. *Amen.*

157. O Lord Jesus Christ, who art the way, the truth and the life; we pray thee, do not permit us to stray from thee, who art the way, to distrust thee, who art the truth, nor to rest in any other thing than thee, who art our life. Teach us by thy Holy Spirit what to believe, what to do, and wherein to take our rest. For your own name's sake we ask. *Amen.*

LIGHT

158. Lord, the darkness, like a jungle, closes in upon us, and without newness of light and life our battle is lost. Forbid that we should be content to curse the darkness. Help us to keep the fragile light of faith alive; through Jesus Christ our Lord. *Amen.*

FOR SEEKERS

159. As we seek for wisdom and understanding, O Lord our God, may our search lead us to you and to your storehouse of grace. May all our seeking be done honestly and reverently, that when our minds are perplexed and our spirits troubled, we may carry on patiently with our daily obligations and be ready to receive you when you come to us: through Jesus Christ our Lord. *Amen.*

160. Almighty God, we thank that you have blessed us with an abundance of questions and a poverty of answers. Deliver us from the arrogance of

knowing all the answers, and goad us with the urge to be wise seekers. Open our minds, kindle our imaginations, and so channel our wills that we may persevere in our seeking until we behold our Savior face-to-face; through the same Jesus Christ our Lord. *Amen.*

THE LOVE OF CHRIST

161. O Lord Jesus Christ, by your works of love
You have shown us the love of God in all its saving
    power;
Now help us,
Who have received beyond measure from your love,
    to have the grace
To trust your love never to fail us,
And so to give ourselves
In love that is pure, and strong, and saving,
To our neighbors, in their need. *Amen.*

DEDICATION

162. Freely, O Lord, we acknowledge your goodness.
You rule your creation by right,
And freely we accept your direction.
Direct us, O Lord, in all we do.
And give us the help of your Spirit,
That what by His teaching we know to be right,
We may, by His might, perform. *Amen.*

SAINTS

163. God, you have called us to be saints. Teach us that not all saints are trapped in church windows or weathering in the deep cold ground. Enable us to fulfill our calling. Infuse us with that persistent and radiant faith which finds expression in action; through Jesus Christ our Lord. *Amen.*

FOR THE UNITY OF THE CHURCH

164. O God and Father of us all, you have called us into a holy unity in the fellowship of your church; forgive our unhappy divisions and restore the visible unity of your church. Make us one in love and faith and service. And grant that we may again be reunited in the apostles' teaching and fellowship, in the breaking of bread and the prayers, and by your blessing and grace, enable us always to keep the unity of the Spirit in the bond of peace. *Amen.*

PREPARATION FOR THE HOLY COMMUNION

165. Lord teach us how to pray and how to live. Grant us a full and continuing part in the fellowship of those who love and obey you. Enable us with glad and generous hearts to share our daily bread, and when we gather to worship you in the breaking of bread, to lift up our hearts in thanksgiving; through Jesus Christ our Lord. *Amen.*

GENERAL PRAYERS

166. With grateful hearts, O Lord, we praise you for all true and faithful witnesses. You have surrounded us with a great cloud of faithful persons and signs which tell of your wondrous acts and give testimony to your great mercies.

For all who speak for you in the face of the world's indifference or ridicule, we thank you. May they continue to reveal your way in the midst of our confusion and blindness. May they give voice to the true needs of our souls even when we forget that we are your children.

We bless you for men and women of all kinds and stations who have been eyes to our eyes and ears for our hearing. When we have turned from your living Word, they have called us to listen. When we have walked in darkness they have carried the lantern of your truth before us.

We pray you to bestow the light of your grace upon all who witness for you by the written page. For artists and singers who praise you, make us grateful. For every tree and spire which lifts our vision to higher things, for every face alive with trust and high resolve, we give thanks.

Lord, make us all walk in the company of this great cloud of witnesses that we may run with perseverance the race that is set before us, looking to Jesus the pioneer and perfecter of our faith. And to him be all glory and honor. *Amen*.

167. Eternal God, today we take up all of the duties and affairs of our lives, grateful for the inspiration and the renewal of life which you make available to us. Help us to remember that all days belong to you. May we honor you by the way in which we do our work and discharge our responsibilities in our homes and in our community. Grant that our love for you may show itself in respect for the worth and dignity of others.

As you have given us this day, give us also, we pray, wisdom and strength to meet the experiences which it brings. Help us to keep the hours unmarred by thoughtless words and unkind acts. Banish fears and anxieties from us and give us faith which finds in you the source of healing for body and soul. Give us courage to stand for your truth, and the willingness to sacrifice comforts and privileges that your kingdom may come among us. These prayers we offer in the name of our Savior, Jesus Christ. *Amen*.

OFFERTORY SENTENCES AND PRAYERS

168. Do not say to your neighbor, "Go, and come again, tomorrow I will give it"—when you have it with you (*Proverbs 3:28*).

Give us the Spirit of Service, O God our Father, so that none may want, but each according to his need may share your bounty, for the love of your Son, Jesus Christ our Lord. *Amen.*

169. If the readiness is there, it is acceptable according to what a man has, not according to what he has not (*II Corinthians 8:12*).

Give us grace, O Lord, to be truly thankful for your many mercies, and make us ready to use everything you give us to accomplish your purposes. *Amen.*

170. You will be enriched in every way for great generosity, . . . for the rendering of this service not only supplies the wants of the saints but also overflows in many thanksgivings to God (*II Corinthians 9:11-12*).

Bind, O God, the heart of every man to his neighbor, and the hearts of all men to you, in whom the whole family in heaven and earth are one, through Jesus Christ our Lord. *Amen.*

171. In all things I have shown you that by . . . toiling one must help the weak, remembering the words of the Lord Jesus, how he said, "It is more blessed to give than to receive" (*Acts 20:35*).

Lead us from the dead-end alleys of our self-interest, Lord, to the broad avenues of your redeeming charity, where we may live completely, and be responsive to your love. *Amen.*

172. Each one must do as he has made up his mind, not reluctantly or under compulsion, for God loves a cheerful giver *(II Corinthians 9:7).*

Lord God, because you love the cheerful giver, confer upon us cheerfulness in giving to you, and graciously accept that which we gladly devote to the service of our Master and Example, Jesus Christ. *Amen.*

173. Every one to whom much is given, of him will much be required; and of him to whom men commit much they will demand the more *(Luke 12:48).*

May we meet your requirements, Lord, not as reluctant taxpayers, but as joyful participants. *Amen.*

LOYALTY SUNDAY—EVERY MEMBER CANVASS SUNDAY

174. As each has received a gift, employ it for one another, as good stewards of God's varied grace *(I Peter 4:10).*

May these gifts and promises of support make it possible for _____ Church to be faithful to your calling and responsive to your leading, we pray in Jesus' name. *Amen.*

ADVENT

175. And from his fulness have we all received, grace upon grace. For the law was given through Moses; grace and truth came through Jesus Christ *(John 1:16-17).*

As by these tokens we mark ourselves as your servants, Lord, may we be faithful in the use of this life and all its things. *Amen.*

CHRISTMAS

176. For the grace of God has appeared for the salvation of all men, training us . . . to live . . . godly lives in this world, awaiting our blessed hope, the appearing of the glory of our great God and Savior Jesus Christ, who gave himself for us to redeem us from all iniquity and to purify for himself a people of his own who are zealous for good deeds *(Titus 2:11-14).*

O God whose grace appeared in the coming of Jesus for the salvation of all men, may these gifts of ours today be true signs of our pure zeal for good deeds. *Amen.*

LENT

177. For God so loved the world that he gave his only Son. Beloved, if God so loved us, we also ought to love one another *(John 3:16, I John 4:11).*

Accept these gifts, O Lord, as our recognition that we have been ransomed at the highest cost, that we may live no longer for ourselves, but for him who loved us and gave himself for us, Jesus Christ our Lord. *Amen.*

PALM SUNDAY

178. [Jesus said:] If any one serves me, he must follow me; and where I am, there shall my servant be also; if any one serves me, the Father will honor him *(John 12:26).*

Lord, as the faithful disciples of your son spread their garments in the way and covered it with branches, so may we lay at his feet all that we have and are, and bless you, in whose name and by whose mercy he came. *Amen*.

EASTER

179. Blessed be the God and Father of our Lord Jesus Christ! By his great mercy we have been born anew to a living hope through the resurrection of Jesus Christ from the dead (*I Peter 1:3*).

In gladness we receive the gifts of new life, Lord; and in gladness we give ourselves and what we have to serve your loving will. *Amen*.

PENTECOST

180. Now we have received not the spirit of the world, but the Spirit which is from God, that we might understand the gifts bestowed on us by God (*I Corinthians 2:12*).

Lord, give us your Holy Spirit in ever greater depth, that we may receive the full treasure of all your gifts. *Amen*.

GENERAL

181. Almighty God, we pray that these offerings may be used for the glory of your name. In the proclamation of the gospel, the confirmation of your church, and the coming of your kingdom, through Jesus Christ, our Lord. *Amen*.

182. Most gracious God, as we bring our gifts to you, pardon and take away all our lukewarmness in your service. Mercifully deal with us, not according to the poverty of our devotion, but according to the richness of your grace in Jesus Christ, our Lord. *Amen*.

183. O God without whose favor nothing profits, let your blessing accompany these gifts which we offer for your work; and let it remain in our hearts, making us richer, not poorer, for what we have given to you, through Jesus Christ our Lord. *Amen.*

184. Lord, teach us by your Spirit to be thoughtful and prayerful in our giving. Grant us the joy of the generous heart, and the spirit of love and self-sacrifice that was in Jesus Christ our Lord. *Amen.*

185. Accept, Lord, we pray, this offering we make. Cause it to be used to the glory of your name in the work of your kingdom. Teach us to bring, not only gifts, but our whole lives, for your service, through Jesus Christ our Lord. *Amen.*

186. O God, the Fountain of all good; we bring you our gifts, according as you have prospered us. Enable us, with our earthly things, to give you the love of our hearts and the service of our lives. Let your favor, which is life, and your steadfast love, which is better than life, be with us now and always; through Jesus Christ our Lord. *Amen.*

187. Almighty and ever blessed God, who in the abundance of your goodness have given us more than we desire or dare to ask; give us, we pray, a spirit of thankfulness, and increase in us the grace of charity, that we may always be more willing to give than to receive; and so rule our hearts that all we have may be used for your service, and that our lives may be consecrated to you; through Jesus Christ our Lord. *Amen.*

188. Almighty God, because you have not spared your own Son, but delivered him up for us all, and because you have freely given us all things in him; receive these offerings which we bring to you; and enable us, with all our gifts, so to yield ourselves to you, that with body, soul, and spirit we may truly serve you and in your service we may find our deepest joy; through Jesus Christ our Lord. *Amen.*

189. O Lord our God, teach us to give cheerfully of our substance for your cause and kingdom. Let your blessing be upon our offerings, and grant us the joy of those who give with their whole hearts; through Jesus Christ our Lord. *Amen.*

190. O Lord, the Giver of all good; we ask you to behold in these our gifts our consecration to your service. Grant that now and at all times our gratitude may be as great as our need for your mercy; through Jesus Christ our Lord. *Amen.*

PRAYER OF CONSECRATION
AT THE LORD'S SUPPER

191.

Minister: Lift up your hearts

People: We lift them up unto the Lord

Minister: Let us give thanks unto our Lord God

People: It is meet and right so to do.

Minister: It is very meet, right, and our bounden duty, that we should at all times, and in all places, give thanks unto thee, O Lord, Holy Father, almighty, everlasting God. Therefore with angels and archangels, and all the company of heaven, we laud and magnify thy glorious name, evermore praising thee and saying:

Minister and People: Holy, holy, holy Lord God of hosts, heaven and earth are full of thy glory. Glory be to thee, O Lord, most high. Blessed is he that cometh in the name of the Lord; hosanna in the highest.

We give thanks to thee, we praise thee, we glorify thee, O Lord our God, who didst so love the world that thou gavest thine only-begotten Son, that whosoever believeth in him should not perish but have eternal life.

Minister: We thank thee for his holy incarnation and lowly birth, for his perfect life on earth, for his ministry mighty in deed and word, and above all for his precious sufferings and death on the cross, on which he gave himself for us, a fragrant offering and perfect sacrifice unto thee. We praise thee for his glorious resurrection from the dead and ascension to thy right hand in heaven, for his continual intercession as our great High Priest and Mediator, for his gift of the Holy Spirit and for the blessed hope of his advent in glory.

Wherefore, O Father, commemorating the passion and death of thy Son Jesus Christ, rejoicing in his resurrection, and awaiting his advent, we thy servants do set forth this memorial according to his holy institution and commandment, giving thanks to thee for the perfect redemption which thou hast wrought for us in him. And we beseech thee to send down thy Holy Spirit, the Lord and giver of life, to sanctify us and these thy gifts of bread and wine, that the bread which we break may be the communion of the body of Christ, and the cup which we bless the communion of the blood of Christ. Grant that we, receiving these gifts in faith and love, may receive Christ our Saviour anew into our hearts and may together grow up in all things unto him who is the Head; through whom, in the unity of the Holy Spirit, all honour and glory be unto thee, O Father Almighty, world without end. *Amen.*

BLESSINGS AND DISMISSALS

I

192. The grace of our Lord Jesus Christ be with your spirit. *Amen.* *(Galatians 6:18)*

193. Peace be to the brethren, and love with faith, from God the Father and the Lord Jesus Christ. Grace be with all who love our Lord Jesus Christ with love undying. *Amen.* *(Ephesians 6:23, 24)*

194. The God of peace who brought again from the dead our Lord Jesus, the great shepherd of the sheep, by the blood of the eternal covenant, equip you with everything good that you may do his will, working in you that which is pleasing in his sight, through Jesus Christ; to whom be glory for ever and ever. *Amen.* *(Hebrews 13:20)*

195. The grace of the Lord Jesus Christ and the love of God and the fellowship of the Holy Spirit be with you all. *Amen.* *(II Corinthians 13:14)*

II

196. Finally, brethren, farewell. . . . Agree with one another, live in peace, and the God of love and peace will be with you. *Amen.* *(II Corinthians 13:11)*

90

197. Be watchful, stand firm in your faith, be courageous, be strong. Let all that you do be done in love. The grace of the Lord Jesus be with you. *Amen.*
(I Corinthians 16:13, 14, 23)

198. Now may our Lord Jesus Christ himself, and God our Father, who loved us and gave us eternal comfort and good hope through grace, comfort your hearts and establish them in every good work and word. *Amen.* *(II Thessalonians 2:16-17)*

ACKNOWLEDGMENTS

OPENING SENTENCES

Selected by Loring D. Chase from the Revised Standard Version of the Bible, copyrighted 1946, 1952, © 1971, 1973. Used by permission of the National Council of Churches.

PRAYERS

1-13 ....Ernest Gordon

14-16 ....Loring D. Chase

17 ....Horton Davies

18 ....Robert L. Young

19 ....*Book of Worship* of the Evangelical and Reformed Church. Used by permission of Eden Publishing House.

20-26 ....Loring D. Chase

27-29 ....Horton Davies

30-31 ....Alexander Campbell

32-34 ....*An Order of Worship for the Proclamation of the Word of God and the Celebration of the Lord's Supper.* © 1968 by the Executive Committee of the Consultation on Church Union. Used by permission of Forward Movement Publications.

35-37 ....Horton Davies

38 ....William Booth

39 ....Loring D. Chase

40-41 ....Elinor Galusha

42-45 ....Scott Brenner

46-60 ....Ernest Gordon

61 ....Morris Slifer

62-70 ....Selected by Loring D. Chase from the Revised Standard Version of the Bible, Copyright 1946, 1952 © 1971, 1973. Used by permission of the National Council of Churches.

71-72 ....Donald J. Selby

73-74 ....Theodore W. Jentsch

75 ....Donald J. Selby

76 ....Morris Slifer. Reprinted with permission from *Services of the Church*, No. 8, "The Collects for the Christian Year." Copyright © 1969 United Church Press.

77 ....*Prayers for the Christian Year*, Second Edition, published by Oxford University Press, 1952, and used by permission of the Committee on Public Worship and Aids to Devotion of the Church of Scotland.

78 ....Scott Brenner
79 ....Donald J. Selby
80 ....Theodore W. Jentsch
81 ....Donald J. Selby
82-83 ....Friedrich Rest
84 ....Theodore W. Jentsch
85 ....Donald J. Selby
86 ....Friedrich Rest
87-88 ....Donald J. Selby
89 ....Theodore W. Jentsch
90-91 ....Donald J. Selby
92 ....Ernest Gordon
93-94 ....Donald J. Selby
95 ....Morris Slifer
96-103 ....Horton Davies
104 ....Ann D. Lutz
105 ....Ernest Gordon
106 ....Horton Davies
107-113 ....Ernest Gordon
114 ....Horton Davies
115 ....Thomas a Kempis
116 ....Friedrich Rest
117-118 ....*The Book of Common Order,* published by Oxford University Press, and used by permission of the Committee on Public Worship and Aids to Devotion of the Church of Scotland.
119-123 ....Horton Davies
124 ....John Calvin
125-129 ....Ernest Gordon
130-131 ....*Prayers for the Christian Year,* by William Barclay. Published by Harper & Row, 1965, and used by permission.
132-135 ....William Booth
136 ....Theodore W. Jentsch
137 ....Sheldon E. Mackey
138 ....Robert Klepper
139 ....Merl Schiffman
140 ....William Booth
141 ....The Religious Society of Friends in South Africa. Used by permission.
142 ....Paul Strauch
143 ....Kenneth Nye
144 ....Donald S. Hobbs
145 ....William Booth

146 .... Friedrich Rest
147 .... William Booth
148 .... Horton Davies
149 .... Oliver Powell
150-151 .... R. Pierce Beaver
152 .... Scott Brenner
153 .... Morris Slifer
154 .... Ernest Gordon
155 .... Scott Brenner
156 .... Ernest Gordon
157 .... Erasmus
158 .... Scott Brenner
159 .... Ernest Gordon
160 .... Scott Brenner
161-162 .... William Booth
163 .... Scott Brenner
164 .... Morris Slifer
165 .... Scott Brenner
166 .... T. W. Menzel
167 .... William Earl Brehm
168-180 .... Loring D. Chase
181-185 .... Horton Davies
186-190 .... *The Book of Common Order,* published by Oxford University Press, and used by permission of the Committee on Public Worship and Aids to Devotion of the Church of Scotland.
191 .... *Orders and Prayers for Church Worship* (London: The Baptist Union of Great Britain and Ireland, 1960), edited by Ernest A. Payne and Stephen F. Winward, and used by permission.
192-198 .... Scripture sentences from the Revised Standard Version of the Bible, copyrighted 1946, 1952, © 1971, 1973. Used by permission of the National Council of Churches.

Index of Scripture References

Index of Subjects

Numbers refer to selections.